DRIBBLE DRIBBLE

James Schooler

Images by G Lens Creative

ROYSTON
Publishing

BK Royston Publishing LLC

P. O. Box 4321

Jeffersonville, IN 47131

http://www.bkroystonpublishing.com

bkroystonpublishing@gmail.com

Copyright 2022

All Rights Reserved. No part of this book may be reproduced, stored in a retrieval system, or transmitted by any means without the written permission of the author.

Cover and Book Images: G Lens Creative

ISBN: 978-1-955063-88-3

Printed in the United States of America

ACKNOWLEDGMENTS:

All praise goes to God

I first acknowledge my Granny Rosa Lee and Honorable Judge Ben Shobe my grandfather for always believing in me.

To my mom, Cherria Leveston for teaching me to be a strong man.

To my friend, brother, and true believer in me. Herbert "Crook" Tinker been with me through ups and downs.

To G Lens Creative for bringing this dream to life with beautiful illustrations.

In Loving Memory Of:
Rosa Lee Schooler and Ben Shobe

Also in Memory Of:
R.I.P.
Ahmad Price #10
"Never Be Forgotten"

INTRODUCTION:

This book was written to inspire all youth. To always use the love of your supporters and self-confidence to work hard for your dreams . Who knew a grandmother giving her grandson a jersey and a ball would motivate him to reach greatness? Never take for granted the little things you can do to help a child reach their dreams.

This story begins in a place the has produced GOATS but all too often many young dreamers lose that motivation to be a GOAT due to the environment around them. Through the eyes of an only child from the West End of Louisville, KY, it was true and evident that you can either choose the street life or make the right decisions.

Each day would start with a prayer and the constant reminder to DRIBBLE, DRIBBLE and "Keep your eyes up."

DRIBBLE DRIBBLE

Lil Schoo spent every summer with his grandmother. One day his grandmother told him that he will grow and use his special talents for good.

She thought it was time to provide an opportunity to play basketball, since Lil Schoo loved to dribble, dribble, dribble all day in his room.

Lil Schoo loved to dribble and shoot.
He always dreamed of playing the GOATs.
Granny Rosa Lee always said,
"Work Hard" and "Dream Big!"

Lil Schoo's Granny gave him an official NBA basketball and a LaMello Ball jersey. She told him to go practice how you want to play.

Lil Schoo put on his jersey and he dribbled, dribbled, and dribbled every single day until no one could take the ball from him or he never lost the ball. More importantly, Lil Schoo always kept his eyes up.

By focusing on dribbling everyday, Lil Schoo dribbled right around the bad things he might have seen. When people wanted him to do things that hurt people, Lil Schoo just dribbled and dribbled. He decided to always use his crossover when asked to do bad things.

Lil Schoo used his Granny Rosa Lee's inspiration, opportunity, and love for her grandson to become a GOAT of basketball and to always stay focused and use his special talents for good.

Lil Schoo vowed to stay humble, hungry and do things that would bring positivity to his team.

He especially wanted the community that cheered them and him on to be proud. Whenever you feel like you need to make the right choice, keep your eyes up and dribble to the goal.

3 A's in Life are

Academics, Athletics, Arts

C's to Power Them

Consistency, Concentration, Confidence

All My life I Wanted to be a Baller Eat Good, Sleep Good, and I will grow to be taller.

Work hard in school and I will be a scholar. Dribble, dribble, dribble and one dribble closer to being a baller.

About The Author:

Coach Schooler spent many days with his grandmother Rosa Lee Schooler. She was a loving woman that saw a special talent in her grandson and she provided everything she had to make his dreams become possible.

About the Illustrator : G-Lens Creative
IG and Twitter @glenscreative

For more information visit:
http://www.schoolerprepacademy.com

www.ingramcontent.com/pod-product-compliance
Lightning Source LLC
Chambersburg PA
CBHW061401090426
42743CB00002B/100